FIND YOUR JOY

FIND YOUR JOY

A Powerful Self-Care Journal To Help You Thrive

JENNIFER KING LINDLEY

FOREWORD BY SARAH SMITH, CONTENT DIRECTOR OF *Prevention*

HEARST
HOME

IT WILL

ONE TIME, I WAS HEADING TO WORK AND I SUDDENLY PANICKED.

Where was my tote bag? I'd been carrying too many things, and I recalled putting the tote full of important papers on the ground as I waited for the train. I called my husband, then dashed off the train and grabbed the next one going the other way. We reached my original station at the same time—but the bag wasn't there. As my mind raced and I fought back tears, my husband said, "Wait, what bag are we looking for? I thought it was this one," pointing at the tote bag *I was carrying*. I'd had it all along. That's when I started crying. "I'm a mess!" I said. "No, you're stressed," he said. "You need to give yourself a break."

BE OKAY.

Truer words were never spoken, and that's exactly what this book is: a break. We've all had a tote-bag moment, when it feels as if a bucket of water has been thrown on the spark that keeps us going. The way to bring that spark back is to take care of yourself, but I, for one, have a hard time pinpointing how to do that. There are always so many things that need my time and attention! That's why I love *Find Your Joy*. Jennifer King Lindley, one of my favorite writers and thinkers, has consulted top psychologists and happiness experts to discover what the research says we can do to create more calmness and happiness for

ourselves. The result is this brilliant workbook: Each chapter homes in on a different aspect of a joyful life, such as self-compassion, mindfulness, and gratitude—and guides you through exercises to bring out your best. You can write in this book, and I have found that spending time with it is calming to the mind and invigorating to the spirit.

So give yourself a break, literally and figuratively. Use this book to focus on your inner self and find more joy in the journey of life. You deserve it.

— **SARAH SMITH**

FEELING

OF COURSE YOU ARE. WE LIVE IN NERVE-JANGLING TIMES.

Blame our ever-present phones—which, like babies, demand our constant vigilance even when they're not actually wailing—our ever-winding to-do lists, and the alarming cable news crawl. We now spend endless hours staring at screens, crowding out activities that sustained humans' mental health for millennia: sharing a leisurely laugh around the kitchen table, losing ourselves in nature for carefree hours, or letting our minds wander playfully as we stare at a swirl of dust motes.

But take a deep breath and hear this: Happiness is not something that

STRESSED?

happens only when life is stress-free (is it ever?). Experts in the fields of positive psychology are finding ways we can actively lift our moods by adopting simple practices: savoring small pleasures, practicing mindfulness, renewing close connections, and more. In time, these habits create an upward spiral. The boost of positive emotions they deliver allows you to think more freely and creatively so you can face your daily challenges, large and small, with new resources.

Think of this guide as a sampler of this new science of feel-better habits.

The practices in this journal have been studied by leading researchers. Through simple exercises and thought-provoking writing prompts, you can take each for a test drive and see which ones you find most helpful. Work this book from start to finish or dip into a topic as your mood dictates. Either way, we hope you will stick with it, returning to work on *something* daily until practicing this kind of self-care becomes your routine.

Taking time to develop these happiness habits will do more than help reduce your stress. It can also help you grow and, we hope, flourish.

CHAPTER 1

BEFRIEND YOURSELF

YOU MAY BE A WONDERFUL FRIEND to others in need of emotional support, the first one at the door with a kind word or an emergency quiche. But are you way too hard on another important person—yourself? Do you catch a glimpse of your reflection in the mirror and scowl, or make a small mistake at work and berate yourself mercilessly? "We think all this self-criticism must be necessary to motivate us toward self-improvement," says Emma Seppala, Ph.D., a director of Stanford University's Center for Compassion and Altruism. But in fact this constant harangue takes a heavy physical and mental toll: Harsh self-critics are more likely to suffer from depression and anxiety. "When you experience strong negative feelings, it can feel like an actual threat, flooding the body with stress chemicals in response," explains Seppala. "It just backfires."

NOW CONSIDER A RADICALLY DIFFERENT APPROACH: self-compassion. "It's treating yourself with the same care and concern you would a loved one," says Kristin Neff, Ph.D., a psychology professor at the University of Texas at Austin and a pioneering researcher in this field. It's a simple yet powerful idea. More and more studies are linking the practice of self-compassion to everything from better sleep to a reduction in the body's reactivity to stress. So next time something distressing happens, whether it's big (you suffer a painful breakup) or small (you blow your diet by stress-eating that big bag of chips down to the dust), don't kick yourself when you are down. Instead, acknowledge your discomfort and offer yourself the same much-needed kindness you would offer a friend: *Wow. This is hard! I understand.* It's not making excuses, insists Neff; it's giving yourself the emotional support you need to bounce back.

Self-compassion is also about realizing you are not alone, says Neff. Despite your rosy Instagram feed of other people's tropical cruises and beaming families, life isn't perfect for anyone. Everyone makes mistakes. Everyone suffers losses. You are not the outlier screw-up. Reminding yourself of that truth can turn your feelings of isolation during difficult moments into ones of deep connection, says Neff.

Start showing yourself more love now.

Write about a problem you are currently struggling with.
How are you describing the problem to yourself?

Now shut your eyes and imagine a close friend going through
the same problem. Write down what you would say to that person.
What encouragement and support would you offer?

....

....

....

....

....

....

....

....

....

....

REFLECTION

Were you kinder to your imagined friend than you are to yourself?
Don't you deserve the same care?

What is a shortcoming or imperfection you regularly beat yourself up for? Reflect on how this perceived flaw has made you a stronger, kinder, or wiser person.

....

....

....

....

....

....

....

....

....

TRY THIS

Hold a steadying hand over your heart for a minute or two. "This simple gesture can change how you relate to yourself, providing the same calming reassurance a friend's touch would," says Neff. If you're in a stressful meeting and want to play it cool, hold one of your hands with the other or cross your arms and give yourself a surreptitious hug.

My Self-Care First Aid Kit

You know how comforting it feels to have a friend bring you a steaming cup of tea when you are down. What are some kindnesses you can show yourself when you need a lift? Be generous with your pampering: One 2016 study found that taking breaks for small pleasures during the day could increase productivity.

Fill in the blanks below with your favorite go-to soothing activities.

1. TAKE A WALK IN THE SUNSHINE
   ....

2. PUT ON MY COMFIEST SLIPPERS
   ....

3. BAKE SOMETHING DELICIOUS FROM SCRATCH
   ....

4. ....

5. ....

6. ....

7. ....

8. ....

9. ....

10. ....

Sometimes being a true friend to yourself requires you to be fierce. Write about a time when you bravely stood up for yourself.

....

....

....

....

....

....

....

....

....

....

....

....

....

....

....

TRY THIS

Repeating a mantra during difficult moments can help ease overwhelming feelings and bring you back to the present. Neff recites these words to herself:

"This is a moment of suffering. Suffering is part of life. May I be kind to myself in this moment. May I give myself the compassion I need."

You can adopt her mantra or make up your own kindly go-to phrase such as *"It's OK, I'm here with you,"* *"I'm sorry you are having a tough time."*

"YOU ARE YOUR BEST THING."

Toni Morrison

Get into the habit of catching and correcting your harsh self-talk.
In time, this can make self-compassion your new default.
What self-critical thoughts popped into your head today?
Fill in a thought bubble when you catch one.

What is a more supportive way in which you could have talked to yourself? Fill in the thought bubble with the corresponding color with a kinder alternative.

What caring thing have you done for yourself lately? Write yourself a lovely thank-you note. Be sure to address yourself by name.

DEAR

Affectionate Breathing

Spending a few minutes practicing this exercise is a natural way to soothe yourself, says Neff.

1. Take three slow, deep breaths through your nose.

2. Let your eyelids close gently.

3. Now pay attention to your breath, wherever you can feel it most easily: whooshing through the tip of your nose, in the movement of your abdomen in and out.

4. If your mind wanders, gently return to your breath as if you were redirecting a wandering child.

5. Feel your whole body breathe with the rising and falling of the breath, like the movement of the sea.

6. Allow your body to be rocked by your breath, back and forth, like a baby being soothed.

7. When you are ready, slowly and gently open your eyes.

CHAPTER 2

REVISE
YOUR
STORY

THINK OF YOUR LIFE AS A STORY.
You are both the main character *and*
the narrator—living through events
and interpreting them to yourself as
you go. The problem: That inner voice
may be giving you the most deflating
interpretation possible. Your friend
hasn't texted back, so you tell yourself,
She clearly doesn't care about me! Or
you blow one small deadline and think,
My boss will fire me! Over time, this
habit of negative self-talk can become
"a well-worn pathway, the place your
mind goes most easily," says Ashley
Kendall, Ph.D., a clinical psychologist
and researcher in Chicago. Not only
does this gloomy narrative depress
your mood, but it also makes you less
likely to *act* in positive ways, Kendall
says. "If you tell yourself you're
unlikable, for instance, it affects your
behavior. You may be less inclined to
reach out to another friend. That just
reinforces your negative belief about
yourself. It's a downward spiral."

WHAT IF YOU ADOPTED
A NEW MENTAL HABIT?
Try interpreting your experiences

from a more realistic—maybe
even optimistic—perspective.
As a cognitive behavioral therapist,
Kendall teaches clients to question
the veracity of their negative
thoughts and revise them as needed.
You can try this too. "It's not about
whitewashing the situation or giving
yourself assurances you don't believe.
Instead, you are fact-checking your
worries," she says. One way to do so:
Try to come up with three reasonable
explanations that don't support your
fearful spin on your situation. Could
that currently silent friend be crazy-
busy, or waiting for you to contact *her*,
or have written a note and forgotten
to hit Send? Learning to make this
mental shift can help you feel more
empowered, which in turn will give
you the confidence to act that way.
"It's a lot like lifting weights. Doing it
once is not going to make you buff. You
need to keep at it. In time, your brain
will rewire to create more positive
pathways," says Kendall.

*Now is the time to start revising
your story for happier endings.*

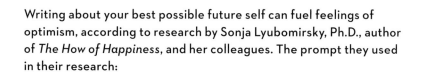

Writing about your best possible future self can fuel feelings of optimism, according to research by Sonja Lyubomirsky, Ph.D., author of *The How of Happiness*, and her colleagues. The prompt they used in their research:

Imagine yourself in the future, after everything has gone as well as it possibly could. You have worked hard and succeeded at accomplishing all of your life goals. Think of this as the realization of your life dreams, and of your own best potentials.

Describe your own future awesomeness in words or even draw a picture.

It's important to remember to search for the silver lining.
Write about a life event that seemed difficult at the time but that
you now realize was a gift.

....

....

....

....

....

....

TRY THIS

When facing a stressful situation, talk to yourself about it in the third
person. Researcher Ethan Kross, Ph.D., a professor of psychology at
the University of Michigan, asked research subjects to prepare to give
a short speech. One group was instructed to talk to themselves about
the task in the first person, using "I" (*I am going to throw up!*). The other
group was told to talk to themselves from the viewpoint of another
person (*Jen will walk to the podium, shoulders back*). Those who
adopted the third-person perspective were calmer and more confident
while presenting. Talking to yourself in the third person allows you to
view your situation with more detachment, allowing your rational brain
to kick in.

"THERE IS NOTHING EITHER GOOD OR BAD BUT THINKING MAKES IT SO."

William Shakespeare

Morning can be the witching hour for anxiety. You wake up to a piercing alarm and start fretting over the day's to-dos. Instead of starting the day stewing about what could go wrong, list five things that could possibly go right today.

1. ....
....

2. ....
....

3. ....
....

4. ....
....

5. ....
....

TRY THIS

Ready to leave a worry behind? Walk through a doorway. According to scientists at the University of Notre Dame, the act of passing over a threshold cues the brain that you're finished with the situation at hand and ready to move on to something new.

Write about a worry here. (Really go for it! Lay on the terrible!)

What are the actual facts of the situation?

....

....

....

....

....

....

....

When you consider the facts, what's a more reasonable perspective
you could take on it?

....

....

....

....

....

....

Our anxieties tend to ambush us at night when we don't have the daytime's bustle to distract us. List three top worries that are no longer allowed anywhere near your pillow.

1. ....

2. ....

3. ....

Good! Now write three happy thoughts you can mull in the wee hours instead.

1. ....

2. ....

3. ....

TRY THIS

Flooded with bad feelings? In *The Happiness Trap*, psychologist Russ Harris recommends describing your emotion (*I am lonely*) to yourself as a temporary state (*I am feeling lonely*). Take it one step further with a little zaniness: Harris suggests singing your statement (*I am lonely*) to the tune of "Happy Birthday." Or try belting it out in a cartoon character's voice. Even if you can't carry a tune, this distancing technique will help you remember that feelings are fleeting and don't define you.

"THERE ARE ALWAYS FLOWERS FOR THOSE WHO WANT TO SEE THEM."

Henri Matisse

Write the short story of your life in which you are a hero who is growing stronger by facing obstacles in your path.

....

....

....

....

....

....

....

....

....

TRY THIS

It's easy to leap to worst-case scenarios, or do what psychologists call *catastrophizing*. Instead, visualize yourself dealing with a problem head-on and resolving it successfully. After all, if you can't fathom what the best-case scenario would be, achieving it becomes more difficult, says Rallie McAllister, M.D., M.P.H.

A mantra of resilience can keep runaway thoughts in check. When you catch yourself fretting needlessly, rebuff the thought by repeating a motto to yourself such as, "*Whatever happens, I can cope.*" Compose your personal motto and write it in huge letters below.

CHAPTER 3

LET IT
GO

WE WILL ALL SUFFER SLINGS AND arrows. Other people ghost us, diss us, disappoint us, wound us. It all hurts, of course. Our natural reaction may be to nurse these slights for days, years, or sometimes decades. "Negative emotions evolved earlier than positive ones and have a tighter grip on our attention. It's a survival mechanism: If you remember when someone has hurt you, you know to avoid them. It could keep you safe in the future," explains Loren Toussaint, Ph.D., a professor of psychology at Luther College. "So your hurt hangs around and holds on tightly."

Although we come by it naturally, this resentment takes a heavy physical and mental toll. "When you hold a grudge, you ruminate—think about the event over and over, trying to figure it out," says Toussaint. Stewing over wrongs both big and small erodes your sense of well-being and can raise levels of the stress hormone cortisol. "There's a tremendous cost to holding on to bitterness, including increased levels of depression and anxiety," he says.

THE REMEDY IS A PRACTICE BOTH SIMPLE AND IMMENSELY CHALLENGING: forgiveness. "It's not condoning what the other person did or abandoning the need for justice. It's simply letting go of the corrosive feelings you have toward the person," Toussaint says.

Resentment is heavy, after all. You will feel lighter and freer if you can put it down. Indeed, one of Toussaint's recent studies found that people who were more forgiving slept better and longer. They also reported better physical health and rated themselves as being more satisfied with life.

If steam is currently wafting out of your ears, where do you begin? "Empathizing is a key to forgiveness," says Toussaint. "Can you put yourself in the other person's shoes? When someone does something to us, we take it personally, but often it is a matter of circumstances. Is it possible this was just a good person in a bad situation?" You might not immediately be ready to let bygones be bygones, but empathizing can start a gradual process of letting go, he says. Toussaint's research has found that pausing for a few minutes of meditation can put you in a more forgiving state too—useful first aid for the wounds from small day-to-day barbs.

It's time to let it go.

Write a letter to someone who hurt you. You don't need to send it—
it's for you. How were you affected by the person's actions? What do
you wish he or she had done instead? If you feel you can, state that
you forgive the person (but don't force it).

DEAR

....

....

....

....

....

....

....

....

....

....

....

....

Difficult people in our lives can test what we are made of. Our conflicts with them help us learn and grow. (For evidence, see every great novel ever written.) Reflect on what your experience with a difficult person in your life has taught you.

....

....

....

....

....

....

....

....

TRY THIS

Loving Kindness is a form of Buddhist meditation that allows you to send your goodwill out to others. To practice it, think of someone you love, someone you don't like, or even a stranger on the street. Repeat the following words to yourself silently as you direct your thoughts toward that person: *May you be happy. May you be safe. May you be healthy. May you be at peace.*

When one door closes, another door opens. Write about how an ending or a failure created new possibilities for you.

Think of someone who you believe is totally different from you, who sparks your intolerance, maybe even your ire. Reflect about one important thing you *do* have in common. Focusing on this commonality can start to bridge divides and make you see the other person's humanity.

Are you reliving a recent small sting over and over?
That keeps your body in a state of stress. Get into the habit of overwriting such thoughts with a memory of a recent kindness.

SMALL STING	KINDNESS BALM

TRY THIS

If you need to apologize for a transgression, use best practices.

Focus on the other person's feelings, not on how bad *you* feel. Jennifer M. Thomas, Ph.D., a psychologist in North Carolina and coauthor of *When Sorry Isn't Enough: Making Things Right With Those You Love*, favors opening with "I apologize" instead of "Sorry." "'Sorry' is a very vanilla word—we use it every time we bump into someone's cart in the supermarket," she says.

When apologizing, state how much you regret what you did. Don't try to justify your bad behavior with excuses. Also, apologize as soon as possible after the incident and do it in person if you can (not through a cowardly text).

A good model: *"I apologize for snapping at you during our meeting this morning. I was totally out of line. I can understand why you would be upset about how I acted."*

No one sails through life without screwing up sometimes. Forgive yourself. Write yourself a failure permission slip below.

THIS ENTITLES MORTAL HUMAN

....

TO REALLY MESS UP AT

....

....

....

AS PART OF THE CURRICULUM CALLED LIFE.

TRY THIS

Are you beating yourself up for being less than perfect? We tend to feel as if we are the outlier if we blow it, so we keep our failings to ourselves. Instead, make a point of sharing your mistakes with others. "You will start to see that errors are common and people are not judging you as negatively as you feared," says Sharon Martin, L.C.S.W., author of *The CBT Workbook for Perfectionism* and a therapist in San Jose, CA. "It's likely your friends will say, 'That happened to me too! Let me tell you how I screwed up!'"

"FORGIVENESS
DOES NOT CHANGE
THE PAST, BUT
IT DOES ENLARGE
THE FUTURE."

Paul Boese

CHAPTER 4

MAKE IT
COUNT

"HAPPINESS IS LIKE A BUTTERFLY. The more you chase it, the more it eludes you, but if you turn your attention to other things, it will come and sit softly on your shoulder," Nathaniel Hawthorne is said to have declared more than a century ago. Indeed, studies are finding that in contrast to idly pursuing fleeting pleasures, focusing on a purpose is one of the surest routes to well-being. Subjects who report having a strong life purpose have lower levels of depression and anxiety and a reduced risk of heart attack and stroke. Meaning can literally be lifesaving: One 2019 study found that people with a sense of purpose were less likely to die prematurely. "Having a clear direction is much better for you than going through life clutching at a bunch of shiny objects," says Anthony Burrow, Ph.D., professor of human development at Cornell University and director of the university's Purpose and Identity Processes Lab.

Your purpose doesn't have to be to cure cancer or to create world peace. (Though if either is your goal, we totally salute you!) "It's very individual. It might be being the best father you can be, or creating beauty around you," says Burrow. "I think of purpose like a compass. It's a guiding tool that helps me know where to go next. I'm never *at* North. It's also forward-looking: When you have a meaningful life aim, you wake up and think, *There is something I need to accomplish today."*

A SENSE OF PURPOSE ACTS AS A POWERFUL FORM OF SELF-AFFIRMATION, say experts—that's a fancy way of saying "You know who you are." An enduring sense of identity can help you weather life's inevitable challenges. "It's like armor. I know what resources I have to draw from. I know where I am going to land," says Burrow. That may be why people who have a strong sense of purpose have been shown to be physically less reactive to stressors.

So how do you discover your reason to get up in the morning? Burrow asks his study subjects, *What is it that you most want to accomplish or contribute? If you don't have a specific purpose, consider what you might want to work toward in the future.* Even just pondering this confers stress-relieving benefits.

There is power in just asking yourself the question.

What have you created that you are most proud of? Why?

....

....

....

....

....

....

....

....

....

....

....

....

....

....

TRY THIS

Having a sense of meaning is essential for a well-lived life.

That doesn't mean the search for it is always joyful. "We often hurt where we care most," says Steven C. Hayes, Ph.D., a professor of psychology at the University of Nevada, Reno, and the author of *A Liberated Mind: How to Pivot Toward What Matters.*

At the heart of purpose is often risk. In a popular TED Talk, Hayes shared his experience with debilitating panic disorder. During the talk, he had to relive a long-ago moment of terror and actually screamed out loud. "Beforehand, I told my wife, *I just can't do it*. And it *was* hellacious. But I wanted my experience to be of use to others," he says. Since then, he has heard from people around the world who were helped by his candor.

You can use difficult feelings as a guide in your life too. "If you are doing something that reflects the deepest part of you, you open yourself up in the most vulnerable place," says Hayes. You might be helping a loved one through an illness or spending sleepless hours struggling to achieve something you are worried you won't be able to pull off. "To discover purpose, ask yourself where you hurt. Then flip it over. What does that suggest you care deeply about?" says Hayes. "True happiness is being open and aware, able to move toward important things, even when those things are difficult."

Whose life have you influenced, whether in a big way or
in a small way?

What do you want to be remembered for?

....

....

....

....

....

....

How can you do more of that thing now?

....

....

....

....

....

....

....

Create a Vision Board

MeiMei Fox, a life coach based in Paris, encourages her clients to use collages of images that represent their goals, dreams, and ambitions to help them visualize their purpose and tap into their creative sides.

To make your own vision board, Fox recommends the old-school method: Go to an art-supply store, buy a giant piece of poster board, and find images online or in magazines to affix to it. You can also add found objects like an auspicious fortune cookie message.

Look for words and pictures that inspire you, ones that make you go, "Hmmm, I'd like more of *that* in my life." Perhaps you could add a ticket stub from a play that made you cry or a photo of a beach at dawn. "See what story begins to emerge," says Fox. If your vision board has lots of pictures of the outdoors, maybe you're secretly longing for more nature in your life.

Or your design might nudge you toward a new career: Might all those gourmet pictures mean it's time to chase your fantasy of becoming a personal chef? A vision board can help someone who's struggling with burnout imagine—and seek out—a shift in career.

Fox recommends hanging your board on a wall near your bed. That way, she says, "you see it first thing before you go to sleep at night and when you wake up in the morning. It can serve as a visual reminder of what's most important and motivate you to seek out more of it."

REFLECTION

What big themes pop out at you from the images and words on your vision board? How can you spend time today experiencing more of these things that inspire you?

What would you do if you were not afraid of failing?

"THE PRIVILEGE
OF A LIFETIME
IS BEING WHO
YOU ARE."

Joseph Campbell

You have been invited to return to your alma mater and deliver the commencement speech. What important life message do you wish your younger self had known?

Write your life story in seven words. Write them big enough to fill the whole page.

....

....

....

....

....

....

....

"WHAT YOU RISK REVEALS WHAT YOU VALUE."

Jeanette Winterson

Do you ever feel you are neglecting some important aspect of yourself? What is it? How could you get back in touch with it?

....

....

....

....

....

....

....

....

....

....

....

....

....

....

What activities feel most deeply meaningful to you and why?
Reflect on each below.

As a child, what did you dream you would achieve someday?

....

....

....

....

....

Are you there yet?

○ YES   ○ NO

What is one step you can take now to reach that dream?

....

....

....

....

....

CHAPTER 5

BE HERE
NOW

OUR MINDS ARE OFTEN SOMEWHERE our bodies are not. Even during a leisurely stroll, you may find yourself dwelling on regrets about the past (*Why did I have to say that?*) or worried about the future (*Will I ever be able to afford to retire?*) This continuous state of hypervigilance can take a powerful mental and physical toll, contributing to everything from high blood pressure to insomnia, says Elisha Goldstein, Ph.D., founder of the Mindful Living Collective. Not to mention crabbiness—a Harvard study that tracked 2,250 subjects' self-reported moment-to-moment emotions linked mind-wandering with greater unhappiness.

ONE WAY TO QUIET THE CHATTER AND RESTORE PEACE: PRACTICING MINDFULNESS. Rooted in Buddhist meditation, mindfulness has all the more appeal in our frenetic modern world. Think of it as the opposite of multitasking: "You are intentionally giving your full attention to the here and now with fresh eyes," says Goldstein. Where to start? Merely observing your breathing for a minute can pull your wandering, fretful mind back to the probably-just-fine here and now. To do so, focus on sensation: Feel how your chest rises and falls with each breath. Does your abdomen move too? Can you feel cool air entering your nostrils? It's all good. If thoughts intrude (and no worries, they will), just bring your attention gently back to your breathing. "Even five to ten minutes a day can help," says Erin Olivo, Ph.D., a New York City–based clinical psychologist and the author of *Wise Mind Living*. "The more you do it, the more you build the muscle of mindfulness."

You can bring an attitude of mindfulness to activities throughout your day by being aware of your bodily sensations and using all your senses to ground you in your present environment. (Feel your seat on the chair; listen to the hum of the air conditioner.) These little bursts of mindfulness seem to have big benefits. A 2019 study found that squeezing in moments of this informal practice while, say, waiting for the microwave to beep resulted in a measurable increase in positive emotion.

Take a deep breath and start to be here now.

Write about a time you were so immersed in something your worries evaporated and you felt fully and completely present.

....

....

....

....

....

....

....

....

....

....

....

REFLECTION:

Can you do that same captivating activity again today?

Close your eyes and take inventory. What are you feeling in your body right now? Tension? Excitement? Where are these feelings located? Describe your sensations by marking the outline below. Using colored pencils is encouraged!

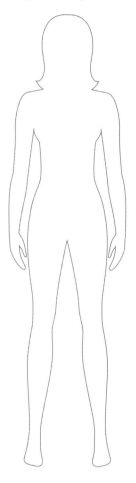

TRY THIS

You can stop your worrying mind in its tracks and bring yourself back to the present moment with this hack, suggests Ashley Kendall, Ph.D., a clinical psychologist in Chicago.

· Look around the room. Count all the rectangles.

· Count all the things with the color red in them.

· Count the number of lightbulbs around you.

Sit completely still for five minutes without doing anything.
What did the experience feel like? Reflect on it below.

....

....

....

....

....

....

....

....

....

TRY THIS

Start the day fully present by making mindfulness part of your
showering routine. Don't spend your time in the steam worried about
your commute (stress!). Instead, notice the warmth of the water on
your shoulders; inhale the herbal scent of your soap; hear the spray
pattering against your shower curtain. If your mind wanders to your
endless to-do list, gently redirect your thoughts by saying a simple
phrase like *Just showering.*

"FOREVER—
IS COMPOSED
OF NOWS—"

Emily Dickinson

What thoughts and feelings are going through your mind right now? Write them one by one in the clouds below. Now imagine you are just observing the clouds with curiosity, watching as they drift away.

"THIS IS A WONDERFUL DAY. I'VE NEVER SEEN THIS ONE BEFORE."

Maya Angelou

TRY THIS

Walk Yourself To Calm

"Walk as if you are kissing the Earth with your feet," says Buddhist monk Thich Nhat Hanh. Indeed, even a short stroll around your block can be an occasion to practice mindfulness. Here's advice for an on-the-go meditation practice from Elisha Goldstein, Ph.D., a clinical psychologist and co-founder of The Center for Mindful Living in Los Angeles. Try one or all of the exercises below next time you find yourself rushing somewhere.

1. As you walk, bring your attention to the sensations of your feet and legs. Notice as your heel touches the ground, the base of your foot, your toes, and then how they feel when you lift them. You can actually say to yourself, *"heel, foot, toes, lift."*

2. Open your awareness to all your senses, one by one: Observe the scene around you. Listen to birds or honking horns. Taste the air. Feel the warmth, coolness, or breeze on your cheeks. Smell the air. Then stop for a moment, and try to take in all of these senses at once.

3. Recite a simple saying as your walk: *"Breathing in, I calm my body, breathing out, I relax."* Or create your own calming phrase.

CHAPTER 6

BOND
WITH
OTHERS

YOU MAY HAVE HUNDREDS OF Facebook friends or legions of Instagram followers. But you can still feel all alone. A 2018 survey found that half of Americans reported suffering from painful feelings of loneliness. We instinctively crave IRL connection, after all: "We are social animals. When we are around trusted others, we feel safer," explains Julianne Holt-Lunstad, Ph.D., a psychology and neuroscience professor at Brigham Young University. Not having a pack around us puts our nervous system on high alert. That may be why lacking strong social ties carries the same risk as smoking 15 cigarettes a day and is riskier than obesity and physical activity, Holt-Lunstad's research has found. "We need to take these relationships as seriously as we do diet and exercise," she says. (No, hitting Like on your friend's dessert photo doesn't cut it.)

In fact, studies have found that people who feel more connected have less anxiety and depression, tolerate pain better, and report higher levels of well-being. (Group hug!) Yet too often having a leisurely latte with pals drops to the bottom of a crammed to-do list. The obligations of adulting take a toll: After people turn 25, their number of friends starts to drop rapidly, according to research from the University of Oxford. The good news: Quality is more important than quantity. "What is most protective is how you perceive your connection. Do you feel supported? Do you believe they will be there when you need them? Make time for those people who matter most," Holt-Lunstad says.

READY TO FEEL BETTER BY MAKING "WE TIME" A TOP PRIORITY?

Even when life gets crazed, there are ways to squeeze in more feel-better bonding. Build time with close ties into your existing routines, suggests Shasta Nelson, author of *Frientimacy: How to Deepen Friendships for Lifelong Health and Happiness*. "Walk your dogs together, or meet up for your grocery store run." Be on the lookout for "found friends" too, she advises. Proximity and consistency are fertile ground for new friendships, so reach out to the people you already see regularly—say, on the sidelines of your child's soccer games or while volunteering. "Self-disclosure helps build friendships, so start by asking questions about what you have in common," Nelson says. Ask the regular at your community garden, "So what got you interested in growing herbs?"

A new friendship just might blossom.

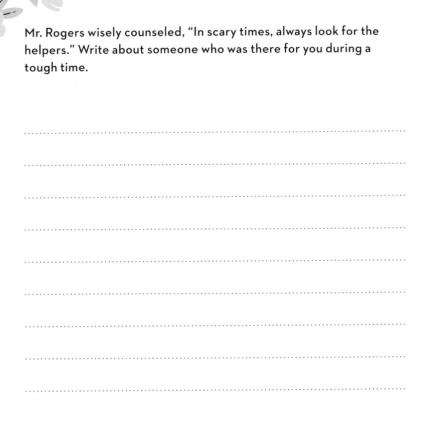

Mr. Rogers wisely counseled, "In scary times, always look for the helpers." Write about someone who was there for you during a tough time.

....

....

....

....

....

....

....

....

....

TRY THIS

Just met a possible new friend? Don't worry about bowling the person over with your wittiest anecdotes. One 2017 Harvard study found that people who asked more questions, particularly follow-up questions that picked up on something the other person said, made a better first impression on new conversational partners.

Who are your favorite people in the world who surround you with support? What does each bring to your life?

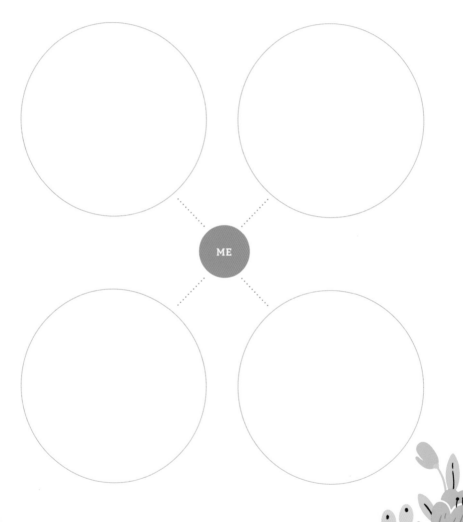

"TO GET
THE FULL VALUE
OF A JOY YOU MUST
HAVE SOMEBODY
TO DIVIDE IT WITH."

Mark Twain

What does family mean to you?

....

....

....

....

....

....

....

....

....

....

....

....

....

....

What do your friends cherish most about you? (Go ahead, ask them!)

TRY THIS

Make a point to talk to not-quite-strangers: the barista who whips up your morning cappuccino, the lady downward-dogging on the yoga mat next to you. Gillian Sandstrom, Ph.D., a psychology professor at the University of Essex in the U.K., conducted a study asking people to count, using clickers, the number of times they talked to such "weak ties" in a six-day period.

The results: The more clicks, the happier people felt. Even these quick hits of connection can increase your well-being and reduce loneliness, she says. (Hint: Dogs make excellent topics of conversation.)

When it comes to having more friend time, be proactive. "Get comfortable being the initiator and reaching out," says Nelson. "Don't view it as giving something to the other person. View it as giving to yourself." Write a list of three invitations you will extend to others this month. (You don't need to whip out the good silverware and start basting; meeting for a walk will do.)

1.
....

....

2.
....

....

3.
....

....

TRY THIS

Create regular rituals with your squad to keep ties tight, says Nelson. "The first Friday of the month is always happy hour, for instance, or the last Sunday is brunch. You feel closer, as you have something to look forward to together. Plus, it prevents good intentions from resulting in endless emailing that eventually sputters out."

First Aid for Loneliness

It's an empty Sunday afternoon. Or maybe you are stuck in a hotel room far away from home with nothing distracting enough on the 500 cable channels.

Make a list of things you can do to feel closer to others when you are feeling disconnected.

1. TAKE OUT A FAVORITE PHOTO OF ME AND MY FRIENDS TOGETHER.

2. SAVOR A WONDERFUL MEMORY INVOLVING SOMEONE DEAR TO ME.

3.

4.

5.

6.

7.

8.

9.

10.

11.

12.

"LET US BE GRATEFUL
TO THE PEOPLE WHO
MAKE US HAPPY; THEY
ARE THE CHARMING
GARDENERS WHO MAKE
OUR SOULS BLOSSOM."

Marcel Proust

CHAPTER 7

COUNT
YOUR
BLESSINGS

SAY THANK YOU! YOU'VE NO DOUBT heard that message since you were old enough to clutch a birthday gift. But gratitude is more than just good manners: It's increasingly being recognized as a powerful form of self-care. Studies have linked living a thankful life to having fewer aches and pains, getting better sleep, and other benefits. "Making gratitude a daily practice is like taking a vitamin," says David DeSteno, Ph.D., a professor of psychology at Northeastern University in Boston and the author of the book *Emotional Success.*

THAT MAY BE BECAUSE GRATITUDE INVOKES A SENSE OF DEEP CONNECTION, say experts: You feel indebted to your partner for the surprise flowers, or to nature for a beautifully crisp winter day. "Gratitude is affirming the goodness in one's life and recognizing that its source lies outside the self," says Robert Emmons, Ph.D., a professor of psychology at the University of California, Davis, and a leading researcher on the topic. In one of his groundbreaking studies, Emmons asked a group of volunteers to write down five things they were grateful for once a week for 10 weeks. (Sample entry: *The sun on my skin.*) Other groups recorded either small hassles or neutral events. At the end of the study, the blessing counters reported feeling 25 percent happier. They also spent 30 percent more time exercising and had fewer health complaints. The sense of profound well-being that washes over us when we are grateful sends a message to our bodies that all is well, quieting our stress responses, Emmons says. "Feelings of gratitude trigger the parasympathetic, or calming, branch of the nervous system."

What about those raggedy days when you are feeling less than blessed? "Gratitude is a choice, and we can create it at virtually any moment in our lives," says Emmons. Doing so may rewire our brains in a lasting way: A preliminary study found that three months after writing a series of thank-you letters, volunteers still showed increased sensitivity in the gratitude-related parts of their brains. Thank goodness.

Start reaping gratitude's rewards.

Get the most from your gratitude journal.

The benefits of keeping a regular gratitude journal are well studied. Some research-backed best practices:

1. Don't just dash off a laundry list of items—stop and contemplate *why* you feel grateful, and be as specific as possible. In one study, people who wrote five sentences about a single positive thing got more of a happiness boost than those who wrote one sentence each about five different things.

2. Look out for little surprises too. We tend to think of the larger categories when considering gratitude: family, home, health. All good! But over time, gratitude focused only on these can lose its impact. Look around for surprising little things to be grateful for (a sudden snowfall, a surprise email from a childhood friend).

3. Whether you keep your record on an app, on slips in a jar, or in a notebook, go back and reread all your blessings when you need a quick lift.

What is something wonderful you never dreamed you'd have in your life today?

What was the best gift you ever received?
(It doesn't have to be a thing.) What did it mean to you?

....

....

....

....

....

....

....

....

TRY THIS

Put the "you" in "thank you," advises Sara Algoe, Ph.D., a psychology professor at the University of North Carolina at Chapel Hill. Her research has found that to build closer bonds, you should express your appreciation with language that acknowledges the giver rather than indicating how the gift makes *you* feel, such as "*You are so thoughtful to remember my favorite color!*" rather than "*I will look great in this scarf!*"

Write about someone who was very important to you as a child. How did that person shape who you are today? How would you express your gratitude to them?

What is something you are grateful for that is small enough to fit in a teacup? Draw a picture of it here.

TRY THIS

Practicing gratitude shouldn't be just one more must-do to fit into your packed list. Instead, build the practice into your daily routine. Meredith A. Pung, Ph.D., a clinical research coordinator at the University of California, San Diego, uses natural reminders. Get into the habit of thinking about something you are grateful for, say, every time you open a door. "I stop several times a day to notice, appreciate, and savor the good in my life," Pung says.

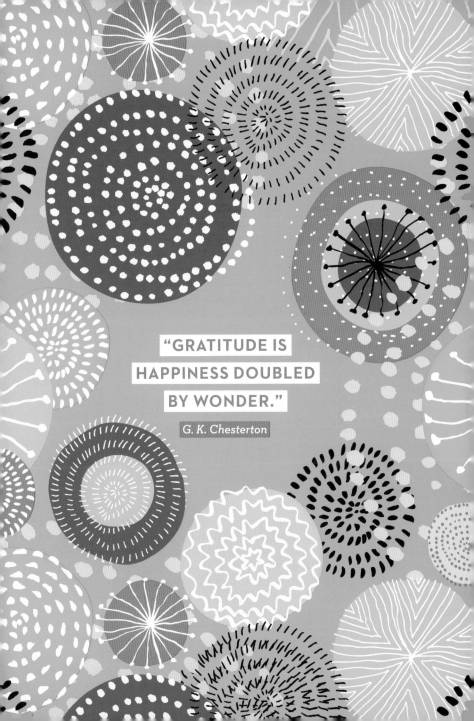

"GRATITUDE IS
HAPPINESS DOUBLED
BY WONDER."

G. K. Chesterton

One way to keep from taking the blessings in your life for granted is to practice what experts call mental subtraction. That's when you consider what your life would be like *without* something or someone.

Think about someone very special to you. How would your life be less rich if he or she had never come into it?

....

....

....

....

....

....

....

....

....

....

....

....

You do have that person in your life! Write about how he or she has enriched your life (and perhaps give the person a big hug the next time you see him or her).

Write about one thing you are grateful for every day for a week.

MONDAY

....

....

....

TUESDAY

....

....

....

WEDNESDAY

....

....

....

THURSDAY

....

....

....

FRIDAY

. . . .

. . . .

. . . .

SATURDAY

. . . .

. . . .

. . . .

SUNDAY

. . . .

. . . .

. . . .

REFLECTION:

Now reread your entries. Such abundance!
You are on your way to a regular habit!

TRY THIS

Write a Letter of Gratitude

Addressing someone who has affected your life in a positive way in a sincere note can boost your own happiness, research shows. And it's a twofer: The recipient of your note will feel good too. So what stops people? "Senders believe receiving a letter like this might feel uncomfortable or awkward for the person they are writing to," says Amit Kumar, Ph.D., a professor of psychology and marketing at the University of Texas at Austin, who researched the question in a 2018 study. (In fact, many recipients described themselves as ecstatic.)

No need to be Shakespeare: Receivers valued the "warmth" of the message over perfect wording. The messages of gratitude in the study were sent as emails (no fancy card stock required), but they still had a big impact. So go ahead, use that stationery, and write that warm note to the sixth-grade teacher who always encouraged you.

"WE CAN ONLY BE SAID TO BE ALIVE IN THOSE MOMENTS WHEN OUR HEARTS ARE CONSCIOUS OF OUR TREASURES."

Thornton Wilder

CHAPTER 8

BASK
IN AWE

WHAT'S GIVEN YOU GOOSEBUMPS
lately? It might be gazing out at the
endless ocean as a lone seal breaks
its surface, his sleek head offering
a glimpse of the teeming mystery
world below. It could be marveling
at the Sistine Chapel, listening to a
soaring piece of music, or witnessing
an inspiring act of kindness. "Awe is
the mind and body's reaction to being
pushed outside of its normal way of
looking at the world," says Michelle
Shiota, Ph.D., an associate professor of
psychology at Arizona State University.
"It stops us in our tracks and makes us
say, 'Whoa!'"

**SUCH MOMENTS OF WONDER
CAN DO MORE THAN TAKE
YOUR BREATH AWAY:**
A growing body of research suggests
that the mysterious emotion of
awe has a range of benefits. In one
study, subjects who reported more
experiences of awe had lower levels
of cytokines, proteins that promote
inflammation. Why? Awe shifts our
attention away from the self and
reminds us that we all are part of

something bigger. (Ever peer out of an
airplane at the clouds below and feel
your own problems dwindle?) That
sense of connection and wonder can be
powerfully restorative.

We have all felt awe's stir, but too
often we don't make room for it. "Our
culture is awe-deprived," says Paul Piff,
Ph.D., a professor of psychological
science at the University of California,
Irvine. "We spend more time staring
down at our phones, less time looking
up at the night sky." People often think
that to feel awe, one has to skydive
or go to the Grand Canyon, he says.
In fact, there's opportunity in the
everyday too.

New experiences in particular are
more likely to induce awe, as they
increase the chance that we will
encounter something that will make
us think in new ways. So make a
point of breaking your routine: Take
a detour on your way home to observe
a natural vista, or visit a museum to
see a jaw-dropping exhibit opening.

***Pause and try to cultivate more
wonder.***

Your Awe-sential Must-Do List

The kinds of experiences that tend to elicit the greatest awe are often considered luxuries or dismissed as frivolous hobbies.

"I now see such experiences as essential to my well-being, so I make them a priority and don't feel guilty," says Jennifer Stellar, Ph.D., a professor of psychology at the University of Toronto.

Such big moments can serve you well long after the moment is over: You are creating a treasure trove of positive experiences you can recall in the future.

What's on *your* can't-wait-to-be-bowled-over list?

1. MAKE EYE CONTACT WITH THE MONA LISA.

2.

3.

4.

5.

6.

7.

8.

9.

10.

One of the ways in which researchers elicit awe is to ask subjects to write about experiences during which they felt wonder in the past: Reflect back on a moment when you were amazed by something. Describe it, including impressions from all your senses. What did the experience make you think and feel?

....

....

....

....

....

....

....

....

TRY THIS

Just looking with fresh eyes at the seemingly everyday can make us feel awe, says Shiota. Look at one flower petal by petal, or ponder the mysterious hubbub of an anthill. Really pay attention and take in all its often-overlooked complexity. Try this approach and the lace of frost on your car's windshield, with its delicate symmetry, might amaze you, not stress you out.

Describe the beauty of your favorite season in all its glorious detail.

....

....

....

....

....

....

....

....

....

....

....

....

....

TRY THIS

Give yourself short bursts of awe throughout the day by surrounding yourself with reminders of what you've found mind-blowing. A desk photo of that trip to Yosemite, perhaps, or computer wallpaper of your newborn's face—or you could change your phone's ringtone to a stirring symphony.

Who in your life absolutely amazes you with what he
or she has accomplished or overcome or done for others?
How has that person inspired you?

"WONDER
IS THE
BEGINNING OF
WISDOM."

Socrates

Take a "Forest Bath"

The natural world is one of the most potent sources of wonder. One way to immerse yourself: forest bathing. No, no swimming involved. Rather, participants in this growing wellness practice "immerse their senses and bodies in the ambience of the forest," says Amos Clifford, a naturalist in Sonoma, California, and the author of *Your Guide to Forest Bathing*.

The practice derives from the Japanese practice Shinrin-yoku and has proven benefits for stress reduction: In one Japanese study, researchers found that people who went on a walk in a forest finished with lower blood pressure than those who went on a comparable walk in a city, for instance. Ready to take the plunge?

- **FIND A SERENE SPOT IN NATURE.** It doesn't need to be a forest —beaches, meadows, and mountains are all fair game, as long as "the human-built environment is minimal," Clifford advises.

- **TAKE A "SENSORY INVENTORY."** Feel the breeze, listen to the splash of a nearby creek, watch leaves flutter. Notice which experiences bring you the most pleasure.

- **GO SLOW AND LINGER.** This isn't hiking. When Clifford leads a session, he'll often move as little as 200 yards in three hours. "It's more about being here than it is about getting there," Clifford says.

- **PAY ATTENTION TO YOUR THOUGHTS AND FEELINGS DURING YOUR EXPERIENCE.** "There's no failure in this practice," says Clifford. Simply through being aware of their bodies as they experience nature around them, "people can come into contact with their authentic selves."

Go hunting for awe. Keep a log of all the things that give you goosebumps this week.

MONDAY

....

....

....

TUESDAY

....

....

....

WEDNESDAY

....

....

....

THURSDAY

....

....

....

FRIDAY

....

....

....

SATURDAY

....

....

....

SUNDAY

....

....

....

Lie on your back, stare at the clouds, and ponder your place in the universe. Afterward, record your musings here.

....

....

....

....

....

....

....

....

....

....

....

....

....

....

"ATTENTION, IF SUDDEN AND CLOSE, GRADUATES INTO SURPRISE; AND THIS INTO ASTONISHMENT; AND THIS INTO STUPEFIED AMAZEMENT."

Charles Darwin

CHAPTER 9

EXPERIENCE DELIGHT

YOU KNOW YOU'RE SUPPOSED TO stop and smell the roses (or the hyacinths…or the pumpkin spice…). But who has time with an infinite to-do list and a bleating, buzzing phone? There is a way to put the brakes on the daily bustle and fully experience more moments of joy—a technique psychologists call savoring. "People think when they experience good things, they'll automatically feel happy," says Fred B. Bryant, Ph.D., a social psychologist at Loyola University in Chicago. "But we don't always react in a way that maximizes the benefits." (You might, say, ignore a glorious sunrise as you race distractedly to your car.) Savoring is a way to fully absorb life's joys, big and small. "Through your thoughts and behavior, you can extend and intensify a good experience, extracting every morsel from it," says Bryant.

THE RESULT: NOT JUST MORE DELIGHTFUL MOMENTS, but a boost in your overall happiness levels as well. "Savoring gives you a bigger dose of positive emotion," notes Christine Carter, Ph.D., a sociologist and a senior fellow at UC Berkeley's Greater Good Science Center. "Positive emotions have been shown to reverse the stress response and give us more access to the part of our brains needed for creativity and problem-solving," she says.

The key to savoring is to be intentionally on alert for nice things that happen during your day that you normally wouldn't give a second thought to. When you notice something good, pause and really soak in the moment. Involve all your senses, advises Carter. Bite into a freshly baked croissant from your favorite bakery. Inhale the buttery aroma and feel the delicate flakes melt on your tongue. Pay attention to the pleasant emotions it evokes in you. (*I feel as if I'm back in Paris!*) Scan your body for the physical sensations happiness elicits—for instance, a spreading warmth in your chest. Extending your delight for as long as possible—even just 30 seconds—helps to etch positive experiences deeply into your long-term memory, creating a storehouse of good feeling to tide you through life's challenges.

What if you are more of an Eeyore by nature? "Savoring is a skill like any other—the more you do it, the better you get at it," says Bryant.

Here's how to wring more joy out of your days.

What are three things that gave you joy today?
Describe each in lavish detail.

1.
....

....

....

....

2.
....

....

....

....

3.
....

....

....

....

Train your brain to search out delight. Be on the lookout for three things tomorrow and report back here.

1.
....
....
....
....

2.
....
....
....

3.
....
....
....
....

You savor something all the more if you realize it is finite. (That's why the last day of a vacation often seems the sweetest.) To get into this appreciative mindset, imagine that you are moving next month far away from where you now live. What places and people will you miss the most? Why?

You're staying! Describe your plans to go visit these favorites and what you will relish about the experience.

....

....

....

....

....

....

....

....

TRY THIS

Snap a mental photograph of something that delights you, like your son's face as he whoops over a hockey goal or this summer's first glimpse of the ocean. Compose it carefully—you can use your fingers as a frame. "Try to memorize the way you feel too," says Bryant. "How would you describe the moment vividly if you were showing your photo to other people?" Later, replay those images in your mind to rekindle your positive feelings.

What things give you the greatest joy?
What emotions and memories does each conjure up?

Your very favorite smell in the whole world

Your very favorite taste in the whole world

Your very favorite sound in the whole world

Your very favorite sight in the whole world

Your very favorite touch in the whole world

"LET A JOY
KEEP YOU. REACH
OUT YOUR HANDS
AND TAKE IT
WHEN IT RUNS BY."

Carl Sandburg

Write about a wonderful memory and reexperience
the happiness of it.

....

....

....

....

....

....

....

....

....

....

....

....

....

Sharing happiness with other people is a powerful way to enhance the experience. Write about a time when you helped someone close to you celebrate. *Yippee!*

....

....

....

TRY THIS

Engaging in a short ritual before doing something you like can make your experience even richer. In one study, subjects who were told to unwrap and eat a chocolate bar in a specific step-by-step way savored it much more. So light a candle before curling up in your favorite reading chair, or use a treasured antique cup and saucer for morning tea.

....

....

....

....

....

....

....

....

....

CHAPTER 10

POWER
UP

IS THAT A CAPE BILLOWING BEHIND you? You may not realize it, but you possess superpowers—what psychologists call signature strengths. One of the founders of the field of positive psychology, Martin Seligman, Ph.D., at the University of Pennsylvania, identified 24 character strengths such as curiosity, fairness, and bravery. (See page 118 for the full list.) These strengths are universal, found across cultures. As individuals, we have them in different measures. "Your strengths are at the core of who you are. Expressing them feels easy and natural. When you are using one, you feel *This is the real me*," explains Ryan Niemiec, Psy.D., educational director and psychologist at the global nonprofit VIA Institute on Character. If creativity is one of your biggies, for example, you may feel transported while painting an intricate watercolor or solving the hall-closet organizing crisis using only old shoeboxes. If kindness is at your core, you can feel most alive when you are volunteering to walk a hound from your local shelter.

DRAWING ON YOUR STRENGTHS FEELS ENERGIZING:
Seligman's research found that when subjects identified their top strengths and made a point of using them in a new way every day for a week, they felt less depressed and happier for months after the experiment.

Maybe you already have an intuitive sense of your own powers. "But research shows that most people are not aware of their best qualities," says Niemiec. If that's you, you can take the free character-strength assessment offered at viacharacter.org. Or reflect on a moment when you did something well or maybe even were downright extraordinary. What was it about you that allowed this greatness?

Once you find your top strengths, make a point to apply them in fresh ways daily. If one of yours is a love of learning, for instance, tackle a fresh challenge at work or take up the oboe at last.

It's natural to obsess about our problems, failures, and shortcomings. But "struggles often hone our strengths," notes Niemiec. Remind yourself that you have the resources inside to cope with it all, thrive, and flourish.

Find your superpowers now.

Which do you think are your biggest strengths? Circle them!

APPRECIATION OF BEAUTY AND EXCELLENCE	KINDNESS
BRAVERY	LEADERSHIP
CREATIVITY	LOVE
CURIOSITY	LOVE OF LEARNING
FAIRNESS	PERSEVERANCE
FORGIVENESS	PERSPECTIVE
GRATITUDE	PRUDENCE
HONESTY	SELF-REGULATION
HOPE	SOCIAL INTELLIGENCE
HUMILITY	SPIRITUALITY
HUMOR	TEAMWORK
JUDGMENT	ZEST

"WHEN I DARE TO BE POWERFUL, TO USE MY STRENGTH IN THE SERVICE OF MY VISION, THEN IT BECOMES LESS AND LESS IMPORTANT WHETHER I AM AFRAID."

Audre Lorde

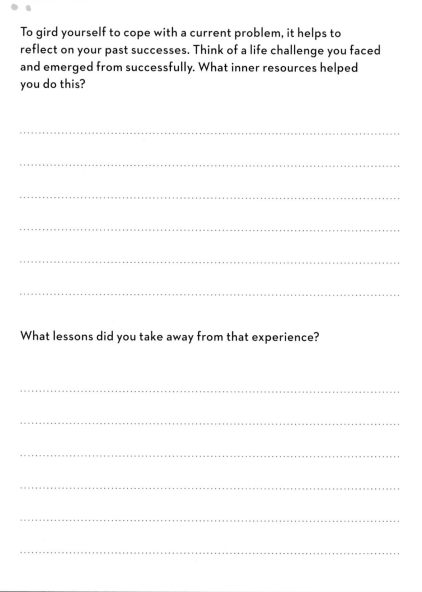

To gird yourself to cope with a current problem, it helps to reflect on your past successes. Think of a life challenge you faced and emerged from successfully. What inner resources helped you do this?

....

....

....

....

....

....

What lessons did you take away from that experience?

....

....

....

....

....

....

Draw a self-portrait below that reflects your best qualities.
(Don't worry about whether it actually looks like you!)

Write about a time when you stepped out of your comfort zone and really impressed yourself.

....

....

....

....

....

....

COMFORT
ZONE

....

....

....

....

....

....

....

Chalk Up Your Daily Wins

Research has found that subjects who spent a few minutes each night writing about what had gone well that day felt measurably happier. "Most of us focus on our weaknesses and on what we don't have," says Carol Kauffman, Ph.D., a life coach and an assistant clinical professor of psychology at Harvard Medical School. "By listing good things, you're training yourself to reverse your focus from what you did wrong to what you did right. You're emphasizing your strengths," she says.

To get even more impact, Beth Kurland, Ph.D., a clinical psychologist and author of *Dancing on the Tightrope: Transcending the Habits of Your Mind and Awakening to Your Fullest Life*, suggests that you share the day's little achievements with a partner or other family member over dinner. Or write your daily small successes on small slips of paper and store them in a jar you keep in view. Once a week, take them out and reread them. "Call up a felt sense in your body of any positive emotions associated with the win—for instance, a sense of calmness or competence. Soak in that experience for a minute or more—really take in the experience," Kurland suggests.

What would your friends or family say you are totally awesome at?

What are you able to do today that you couldn't have pulled off five years ago?

....

....

....

....

....

What has changed in you to make that possible?

....

....

....

....

....

....

....

What is your biggest dream for your future?

....

....

....

....

....

....

....

....

....

....

....

....

....

....

Bon voyage! You are on your way!

"NOTHING CAN DIM THE LIGHT WHICH SHINES FROM WITHIN."

Maya Angelou

HEARST
HOME

Cover design by Kristen Male
Book design by Kristen Male

All Images: Getty Images

Library of Congress Cataloging-in-Publication Data Available on Request

10 9 8 7 6 5 4 3 2 1

Published by Hearst Home, an imprint of
Hearst Books/Hearst Magazine Media, Inc.

Hearst Magazine Media, Inc.
300 West 57th Street
New York, NY 10019

For information about custom editions, special sales, premium and
corporate purchases: hearst.com/magazines/hearst-books

Printed in China

ISBN 978-1-950785-06-3